RSVP
to
Heaven ™

Lee Benton

Lee Benton Ministries International
Laguna Niguel, California

RSVP to HEAVEN ™

Hope Kelley Book Publishing
HopeKelleyBookPublishing.com
800.806.6240

Printed in the United States of America

RSVP to Heaven by Lee Benton

RSVP to Heaven by Lee Benton

This book is dedicated to my precious parents, Lester and Earlene Benton, for always giving me the most incredible love, support, and encouragement throughout my whole life while teaching me to know the true love of God.

~~ Lee

RSVP to Heaven by Lee Benton

Table of Contents

RSVP to Heaven by Lee Benton

Foreword

This book of Lee's is going to change the world because she is changing the world already. Ever since I've known her, she has grown and grown and grown. You cannot grow any more than she has. I am so proud to be a part of her life, and I always will be. I won't leave her for a second. We're going right on from this world to heaven together—to Paradise. We've been best friends since 1982, and our friendship just keeps growing closer and closer as every day goes by. Every single morning, we pray together. That's the way I start my day and the only way I could start it.

~~Terry Moore
(Oscar Nominee, Actress, Producer, Writer)

Introduction

I was inspired to write this book so the whole world would have the opportunity to RSVP to God's Invite to Heaven.

While writing this book, I found myself in the emergency room on May 1, 2022. Due to Covid - 19, my heart went into atrial fibrillation, and I almost stroked out. In the face of death, my dying wish was for three things: for all my family and friends to know how much I loved them, for this book to be finished and published, and for God to please not let me die alone. He answered all three.

The doctors paddled my heart, and God decided my mission on earth was not over yet. I had to get the final edits done for this book to be placed in your hands before my final curtain call.

As an accomplished model, actress and producer of an award-winning TV Show with a worldwide ministry as an evangelist, I first felt compelled to write this book because I see people who are really hurting and suffering, now more than ever. Time is of the essence.

Whether I am traveling for show biz or for the ministry, I see that people want the truth. They need to hear and see it NOW. They also need to know that God has great plans for them, and He has prepared for them a future of hope, not despair!

Personally, I am a non-denominational Christian. I say only what I know is truth, and I want to share it with you. I pray that this book will inspire you to draw closer to God and help you trust Him with every concern you may have. The only way I could have possibly survived and come this far in my life is by the mercy and grace of God.

As the daughter of an evangelist, this PK (Preacher's Kid) took a walk on the wild side for many years. I've always said, "If God can change this rebel, He can change anyone!"

My prayer is that this book not only blesses you but that you will share this with all of your family, friends, and others, so they too, will have the opportunity to pray the "RSVP to Heaven."

~~ Lee Benton

Chapter 1

How it all Began

This prayer was given to me in 2007 by God while I was sitting home alone in my dining room surrounded by my three dogs. As I was reading my Bible, which I do daily, God downloaded this incredible message with a vision about His RSVP to Heaven. After He showed me this incredible analogy, He spoke to me and said that I was supposed to tell everyone this message.

I didn't quite understand how I was supposed to tell everyone, because I am not a person who would stand on street corners holding signs. But God had a plan.

He knew how and exactly when I was supposed to tell the world. It would be revealed and manifested into the natural from the supernatural five years later, in 2012.

I was born and raised in Tampa, Florida, the daughter of Lester and Earlene Benton as "Rosa Lee Benton."

My beloved parents

My Dad, once a cowboy, always a cowboy.

My Father was an evangelist, a former cowboy, a rodeo king, and a World War II United States Army Veteran from Alva, Oklahoma.

My beloved Mother was born and raised in Valrico, Florida. She had such charm and southern hospitality. She was also a loving Sunday School teacher.

My Daddy and me, 1983

My beautiful Mommy and me, 1983

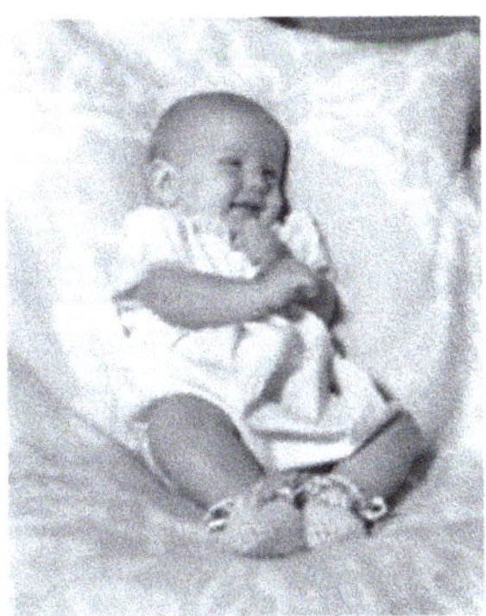

Me as an infant

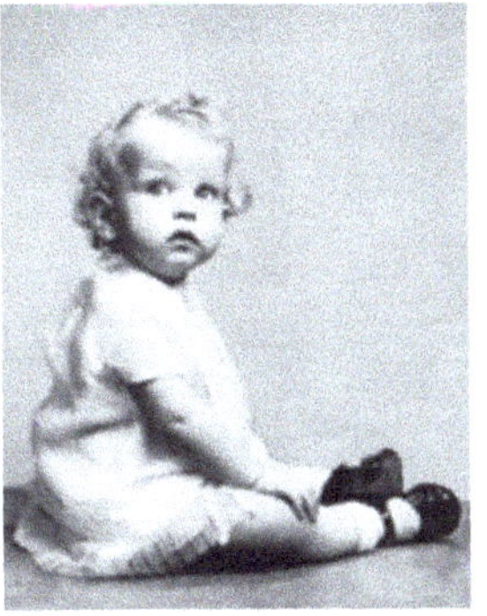

Looking a lot like the
Gerber Baby—check
out my chubby cheeks!

My sister Carolyn and me,
I always looked up to her.

One of my favorites.
Praying with my
sister, Carolyn.

I was chosen from all the schools
in Tampa, Florida to be a Royal Page
for the King and Queen's Court of
Gasparilla in 1959.

High School graduation
photo in 1970.

15

My whole singing career started in Tampa, Florida when I sang gospel songs in church on stage with my older sister, Carolyn. We were known as the "Benton Sisters" and we were booked to sing in other churches and opened for a quartet called "The Messengers."

I graduated from Temple Heights Christian School, a private school, and was a cheerleader for 3 years in high school and head/captain of the cheerleading team my senior year. I was also blessed with the honor of being named homecoming queen.

After high school, I took ballet, tap, and jazz dance, followed by a successful ten-year modeling career. My first modeling agency was Models International, where I met Shelley Abblett. She was a model and also one of my agents who helped catapult my modeling career and later became my best friend.

I eventually began my acting career. After my first two films in Florida, I was *discovered* and brought to Hollywood by an agent, Carol Brewster, at Gerritsen International Talent Agency. She quickly put me under contract in 1982. I didn't know anyone in Los Angeles (L.A.), except my agent, Carol, and my one dear, beloved girlfriend from modeling days, Marilyn Mitchell. Marilyn lived pretty far from me with her husband and child, so I had many lonely days.

These are various modeling photos throughout my career

Top left: First modeling composite

Bottom left: Second modeling composite

Right: Final modeling composite from Florida
that brought me to Hollywood, California

Ben T. Davis Beach
Tampa, Florida

First professional modeling headshot by John Hancock of Models International, 1971

My best friend, model
and agent, Shelley
Abblett and me

Dressed up and so excited to attend the movie premiere of my first role on the film, *Agnes,1974*

Promo Photo: Singing in my first film, *Agnes*, performing as a nightclub singer with my band, *Zapata*, 1974

Phil Lee

Finding my way around L.A. was challenging. I was going on auditions amid the worst storms to hit L.A. in fifty years. It was during a time where there was no   such thing as a cell phone or a car navigator. All I had was a big booklet that mapped out the whole city called a Thomas Guide. I found myself constantly lost amidst all the freeways and millions of streets in L.A., stopping to ask people in the streets, "Can you please tell me where I am, or can you help me find this address?"

This was not fun. I almost gave up acting several times, and I wanted to go back home to Florida. Even though I had a three-page resumé with films, international commercials, documentaries, with a singing and modeling career, everywhere I went producers and casting directors were continually asking, "Where are your L.A. credits?" I wasn't getting the callbacks I had hoped to have.

Another best friend Model/Actress Marilyn Mitchell and me at the Dove Awards in LA in the early '80s

Little did I know that God had a purpose for me to fulfill in L.A. that was greater than my acting career.

Marilyn was an important influence on my life. She prayed for me when I was so far away from the Lord, and she was always there for me. Things changed for me after Marilyn introduced me to the remarkable Matt Helreich, who later became known as "Uncle Matt" to me. He managed some of the biggest stars and knew practically everyone in Hollywood.

Uncle Matt Helreich and my best friend, Actress Terry Moore

Terry Moore and me, 1984

Matt took me under his wings and introduced me to some of the most amazing people, including my best friend, actress and Oscar nominee, Terry Moore.

Terry became like a sister and second mom to me. We eventually started to spend every morning together, reading the Bible and praying on the phone. She is still my daily prayer partner to this day.

My acting career suddenly took off after I had been in L.A. for only three months. It grew rapidly after I

Terry Moore and me, 2022

prayed and reached out to God one lonely night, surrendering my life again to Him. It was a life-changing night. I was miserable, lonely, depressed, and the rain was incessant.

One night, I was sitting alone in my apartment and my TV actually got stuck on Channel 40. Therefore, I was forced to watch this one channel, which happened to be the Trinity Broadcasting Network. I thought they were a bunch of religious fanatics. The more they smiled and praised Jesus, the more I became angry and upset. Then, something majestically, magical happened. The same Holy Spirit that entered me as a young girl started stirring in me whenever they would sing, worship, and praise God on TV.

I found myself standing up, marching around, and screaming out to God, "What do you want from me? My life? Then, TAKE IT!" I continued, "I need to work on TV and films NOW. If I don't, then I will just go back to

Tampa, where all my family and friends love me. If you do this for me and get me work, I make a vow to you, right now, that I will always share on every TV show, magazine or newspaper article, and interview that YOU did this for me."

God took it seriously, and He took it to another level. It was a Saturday night, and that very next Monday morning my agent, Carol, called me and said, "Kiddo, I don't know what's going on, but EVERYONE in Hollywood is calling for you, darling! You've got auditions everywhere. All the studios are calling for you." I wasn't surprised. I smiled and told her I rededicated my life to the Lord. She said, "Wow, it sure worked, because everyone is looking for you." She totally understood because she, too, was a Christian and knew the power of prayer.

I started working immediately on movies, TV Shows, etc. I wouldn't advise anyone to give God an ultimatum like I did, but the Lord had mercy on my ignorance because, as I stated earlier, He knew the plans He had for me.

I had many wonderful years of success after this, starring, guest starring, and co-starring on shows in L.A. My resume became even longer than three pages at this point. After the first year of God opening up all these roles, a dear friend of mine, Bill Shepherd, then the head of casting for Walt Disney Studios, advised me that if I wanted to get bigger roles, I needed to sign with a larger agency.

I took Bill's advice and signed a contract with a larger agency. Immediately, they told me that I needed to change my name to something that was better suited to me. So, I decided to keep part of my name and went from Rosa Lee Benton to "Lee Benton." I started landing much larger roles in television, including soap operas and starring and guest-starring in many films.

Through training and working out with my precious friend, actress, producer, writer, and stuntwoman, Spice Williams Crosby, I met Jacov Bresler, who became my new personal manager. Jacov collaborated with my agent and the Lord's favor grew upon me, helping me to land a series regular role as "Jenny" on Mickey Spillane's Mike Hammer TV Show.

On the set of Mickey Spillane's Mike Hammer TV Show with a few cast members and VIPs (L to R):

William Shatner visiting the set

Jay Bernstein, our Executive Producer

Lindsey Bloom, starring as "Velda"

Stacey Keach, starring as "Mike Hammer"

Lee Benton, co-starring as "Jenny"

Mickey Spillane, Creator/Writer of our show

(Photo courtesy of Sony Pictures)

LOVELY Lee Benton prepares to entertain (left), offers a comparison with her portrait (above) and hides behind a fan (right).

On the set of Mickey Spillane's
Mike Hammer
TV Show as "Jenny"
(Photo courtesy of Sony Pictures)

Spice continued to train me at the gym, and my publicist booked me for many muscle magazines, including the cover of Muscle & Fitness.

Eventually, I had to stop doing muscle magazines. My publicist wanted to position me as an actress who happened to body build rather than a bodybuilder who happened to be an actress.

I continued to experience success in show business for several years attending many Hollywood events, walking the red carpets, appearing all over the tabloids and on many shows and films.

Cover and features for
Muscle & Fitness Magazine
and Excel Magazine, Snyder Productions

My first year in L.A. 1982

Frank Capp

Mindas

Here are some acting headshots, composites, and magazines from Los Angeles, California the '80s and '90s.

Mindas

Minas

LEE BENTON

Mindas

Lee
Benton

Mindas

Mindas and Frank Capp

JACK ROSE AGENCY
A TNT AGENCY
SAG / AFTRA
Lee Benton

I continued to experience success for several years being invited to many Hollywood events, walking the red carpets, all over the tabloids, and starring on many shows and films.

Mickey Spillane's Mike Hammer was number one on the air when our show was cancelled due to losing the leading star of our show, Stacey Keach, who played Mike Hammer. It was hard to carry on a show after losing the leading star. Many of us had invested in new homes, restaurants, and businesses when this happened. The cast was devastated to say the least.

I also found out that my "new agent" with whom I had signed had dropped the ball on my career and failed to promote me after the show was canceled. It felt like the "bottom falling out of my life." I had to pay bills and juggled having a "real job" at a production office and then a law firm while still acting, but not as a series regular as I had hoped.

After all the successes, shows and films, I ended up playing a female Rambo character in a B-minus film after signing with another agent and manager. My manager did not want me to do this, but God had a reason for me to do this. Through this role, my MONDAY NIGHT LADIES SHARE & PRAYER GROUP was birthed on the set right outside of Yosemite. After the movie was over, the other actresses and I decided to continue our share and prayer time together, so I volunteered my condo in L.A. This MONDAY NIGHT LADIES SHARE & PRAYER GROUP became the genesis of my worldwide ministry, as I counseled and prayed with women for years starting in 1990, which was also the beginning of the decade of darkness for me.

Chapter 2
The '90s Decade of Sorrow

Everything I had done with the people I had known, the places I had been, and the great wealth I had earned, not to mention the glamorous lifestyle I had adopted, seemed to spiral out of control.

I had it all, especially with my "Bad Mobile," a term of endearment for my black-on-black, convertible Mercedes sports car. It was gorgeous, all blinged out with wire rims and cherry wood paneling—and it was totally paid off! I had made good money being a series regular and starring in films. I was grateful that I had a car that was totally paid off. I really loved that car, and my gorgeous, long-haired Siberian husky with his big, blue eyes looked so good sitting next to me! We were quite the team together, riding around in the Bad Mobile!

Due to the lack of representation from my new agent, who was literally just sitting on me and my acting career, my wonderful, successful career came suddenly to a halt. I had to use up all my savings from my acting roles to pay my bills. I turned to credit cards to keep up, thinking that surely my agent would get me on another show as a series regular in no time, after Mickey Spillane's *Mike Hammer* had been canceled because our main star of the show had been incarcerated in England with a drug indictment for a long period of time.

But it did not happen. No one had let me know that my agent had left the agency and no one, NO ONE else was representing me at the agency. When I found this out, my heart sank. I had to pay a mortgage, homeowners association fees, home insurance, electric bills, and tons of other bills. At this point, creditors were hounding me. In desperation, I took out a $10,000 loan against my fully paid off, $65,000 Mercedes(today it would probably be worth $150,000), thinking all along I would pay off the loan shark from a local Loan Co. in L.A.

When you get a loan against a car, they take your pink slip. So, they own your car until you pay them off. I thought, surely, I would be back working as a series regular on another TV series right away and be able to pay them and get my car back.

There was pattern a here. This is how many people get entrapped and end up losing their cars. The loan sharks are betting against you to do just that. They can keep your car no matter how far in debt you are. They'll loan you money because the odds are you won't be able to pay the loan off. That's why they're called loan sharks. They're waiting for you to fail and ready to make their money on you. They're betting that you're not going to be able to pay it off.

In the long run, they'll get to keep your car, which is typically worth much more than the loan they gave you. No matter how much you cry and beg for leniency, promise to pay it back, and write promissory notes, none of that fazes them. They are trained to not be affected by your emotions and not to be fazed by your hardship. They want to make money on you, and that's exactly what happened to me. They kept my $65,000 Mercedes. I lost my beautiful car, that was totally paid off, and was left with no transportation overnight for just a $10,000 loan. I was devastated! I had no choice and didn't know what else to do. I had to start working and get a real job. But I needed transportation to get there.

At that time, I had an ex-boyfriend who worked with a car dealership. He had auction relationships and liked that I was in this position of need and groveling. He wanted me to return to him. I wanted to keep going to God and was not interested in re-establishing a relationship with my ex. Since I was not interested in getting back together again, he gave me an old car, a boat-looking piece of junk from a car auction to drive. I was embarrassed and humiliated, but I was grateful, because, when you have no car at all, you are grateful to have any wheels you can get. I was thankful to have a vehicle to get to a "real job" from a real interview (meaning not a showbiz interview) and a source of income. I needed to work, and I was grateful to have wheels to get me there.

I was first hired at a lighting company to do administrative work until the company went out of business and then hired to work for an interior designer in Beverly Hills. The owner was unstable and verbally abused all of his employees. On one of these occasions, I walked out of there and never looked back.

I then interviewed for a production company and worked there for about a year until they closed and moved to their Maryland headquarters.

In the meantime, the former boyfriend, who had helped me out with the first car and knew I needed the loaner, asked to have the car back to sell it. I asked in desperation if he could still help me out with any car because I needed the job, and I needed to be able to drive to make money. So, he came and picked up the car and said he would bring me something else.

What I'm about to tell you is not meant to make you laugh, and is probably the most humiliating and painful thing that has ever happened to me in my whole life. I will never forget the day when he rolled up in a huge, white bread truck. I thought he was playing a joke on me. It was literally a WHITE BREAD TRUCK that looked like a FedEx truck. I nearly fainted from the humiliation and the distress I felt. He said it was all he could come up with to help me right now. I could not believe how my life had come from driving around Beverly Hills in a black Mercedes to driving around in a bread truck. I went into total shock and devastation. I cried, but again, I needed wheels so I could get to a real job and make real money to pay real bills.

I drove that white bread truck for about a week. He must have felt sorry for me or felt I was humbled enough to bring me what looked like a beautiful, black Jaguar. It had a beautiful palomino leather interior and was all blinged out with wire wheels. On the outside it was gorgeous. Under the hood, it was a different story. Little did I know that Jaguars had horrible engines. It was before Jaguars started using Ford engines. Anyone who used to have a Jaguar will know that Jaguar engines were known for breaking down all the time. I ended up in tears all the time, stuck in various places with a broken-down car throughout L.A. Even though it looked beautiful on the outside, it was a piece of junk under the hood. Thank God for friends who had AAA roadside service to help me out because I could not afford it.

From that point, I was hired at a smaller law firm in Westwood because of my administrative skills (thanks God). They thought it was cool to have a TV star at their front desk. There were four lawyers in that office. They were kind and wonderful and easy to work for. Then I got recruited by a person who was from a much larger law firm upstairs while I was riding the elevator. It was a much more elegant office but with an angry, hostile boss. People shook whenever he walked through the office or called in on the phone. At that point, I was sorry I had left the smaller law firm. There were at least fifteen lawyers, and I had to stay on top of all of them. I had to learn to scribe lawyers' shorthand. I found out later that I was working the job of three people, and they were taking advantage of me. I had to learn legal terminology and legal shorthand, and had to make sure it was typed up and sent to their office in Palm Springs. They paid me peanuts to do the job of three people, but still I saw it as money, which was a blessing and necessary in order to live and stay in L.A.

The driving force behind my getting all of these jobs was that I was forced to pick and choose what bills were priority to pay and which ones were of less importance for the month, because I could not pay all of them. So, while I was waiting for my agents to put me in another TV series, I literally was losing money while draining my bank account, trying to keep my head above water.

I had gotten to a point where I really needed food, but I didn't want anyone to know. I remember many trips to the local 99 Cents Only Store. I found out that you can survive at the 99 Cents Only Store with the groceries they have in stock.

Again, coming from a life of luxury, bright lights, and tons of money to this level of poverty while living off the 99 Cents Only Store groceries was beyond anything I could imagine.

That's when I went to a private prayer group hosted by Pastors Jim and Trish Steele. At their prayer group, they had a food pantry where they were offering free food to anyone who wanted it or needed it. I'm not sure if it was pride or embarrassment, probably some of both, that kept me from running to that food pantry.

I was too embarrassed to let people know or let them into my silent storm. I eventually gave in and accepted food graciously from them. I was in such need that I could have taken ten bags of food, but I went away humbly with two bags. For me, it was like Christmas when you don't have any food at all. Again, God was showing up, giving me exactly what I needed just when I needed it.

I think it's important to say that I never wanted my parents, sister, or any family members or friends, to know. I was ashamed, and I did not want to worry them. I knew they would insist that I come back home to Tampa. For me to surrender and go back to Tampa would have been a high sign to everyone saying that I was a failure and that all my dreams and plans in Hollywood had failed. I didn't want them to know that.

It was difficult to keep on top of all my bills, even though I was making money at the law firm. I became so far behind on my electric bill that my electricity was cut off! I was ashamed, embarrassed, and humiliated to let people know that I didn't have electricity for an entire month.

I quickly learned that I could dress in the dark and prepare the outfits in the daylight that I needed for work the next day. I bathed at a friend's place and at a boyfriend's house. My boyfriend at the time was a struggling singer/recording artist, so he couldn't help me. I couldn't stock up my refrigerator because I had no electricity. I couldn't store bologna because I had no electricity. I could wash my hair in cold water, but I couldn't use my blow dryer. It was like camping in my own home. I learned to live in the dark and make sandwiches in the daylight. I could make crackers and ramen soup, but I couldn't heat up my ramen soup. I had no lights. I had no electricity. I had nothing.

I could not tell my family or my closest friends. No one knew how bad my life had gotten and how dark it had turned, literally. I was too embarrassed to let my family, friends, and the world know that this big TV star had crashed and burned. I was driven. I had a crazy drive and endless hope that any minute I'd be rescued and out of this nightmare and be back in my fantasy world of acting.

I was learning to live by candlelight and flashlights for a month. Through all this lack and despair, I managed to keep my job. I showed up to work every day with a smile because I needed to work and make money.

At that point, I had the choice of quitting, giving up on everything including my career and my life in L.A., and moving back to Florida to live with my parents or to stay and start all over again, and keep fighting, surviving, and thriving. I knew if I told my parents, they would be so heartbroken that they would try to come to L.A., pack me up, and move me back. I had to stay and fight! I needed to regain my dignity and self-worth, because at that point, I had lost a lot of confidence in my own identity. I felt like I went from a hero to zero. Yet, I knew I had a purpose. I just did not know the full picture of my purpose just yet.

With no electricity I was faced with a dilemma: Do I tell my ladies at my weekly L.A. Monday Night Prayer and Share Group that I had no electricity and risk having them lose faith when they saw what had happened to me, their leader, or keep it close to the vest and tell them we were going to do something different by having our weekly meeting by candle-light? I chose the latter, and they thought it was pretty cool. Little did they know, I had no choice.

One night, I had chosen to share with the group a little bit of what I was going through. One young actress who attended my meetings fell apart and lost hope and said through tears, "Lee, you're one of the godliest persons I've ever known, and if God allowed this to happen to you, what in the world would He allow me to go through?"

I learned that night that I couldn't share everything with everyone in order to protect them and keep them from losing their faith.

So, on Monday nights I continued to host the meeting by candlelight or reserved the recreation room in my condo complex.

A neighbor who knew I was struggling allowed me to have the prayer group at her condo. For a whole month, I led the prayer group in a different way, and to this day, almost all the women in my L.A. ladies prayer group do not know what I was going through. I was afraid if I let them know, that they would lose faith in God, and I couldn't risk that happening.

Through it all, God was always there to carry me through this, even though it once felt that He had left me. He was there. Even though I had no electricity for a month, an unreliable car, and a harsh boss, I was truly in despair, BUT GOD!

I called the office of my ex-boyfriend who provided me with the previous large car, the big white bread truck, and the Jaguar. I didn't know why I was calling him at his office, but God knew. He was not there, but his boss, a Persian gentleman named Frank Bahadori, answered the phone. I didn't know him personally, but I had met him once or twice before at his business. It was a friendly exchange whenever I saw him with a smile telling him, "It was nice to meet you" or "Hello, how are you doing?"

I was so down and out that when he asked on the phone a simple, "How are you doing?" I totally spilled everything on this man. I cried and told him how bad my life was. He patiently listened, and later I was embarrassed. I told him I had been without electricity for a month. He was very upset and wondered why my ex-boyfriend had allowed this to go on for so long. He had a heart of compassion, and he asked for my address. He said he was going to pick me up to take me to pay the electric bill so they would turn it back on. I couldn't believe my ears! This Muslim man who hardly knew me was going to help me!

Sure enough, he called to let me know he was downstairs, and I quickly ran outside as he pulled up in his beautiful, red Ferrari. He took me to the electric company to pay my bill in person. I could not believe it! God was rescuing me through a total stranger. By this time, I was months in debt to the electric company. This man kept his word. As he was about to pay for it, we went up to the window and he asked, "What is the total that this young woman owes?" She told him the amount, and he paid it with his check right then and there.

As grateful as I was, in the back of my mind, I was thinking and hoping he wasn't expecting any favors in return. So, on the way home, I boldly asked him, "How could I ever repay you?" He told me, "Lee, do not worry about it." I then said, "Why are you doing this for me?" He said, "I understand what it's like to have nothing." He told me that years ago he also lost everything and was forced to be a taxi driver, homeless, and sleeping in his cab. He shared how someone had helped him. So, he wanted to pay it forward, because he said he knew what it was like to have lost everything and have no money at all.

I thanked him a million times, and he probably got tired of hearing it. He had some expensive Persol sunglasses on. I told him his sunglasses looked great, and as if paying for my electricity wasn't enough, this man took off his sunglasses, had me try them on, and told me they were mine. It was a hug from God to make me feel special. Who would have thought this stranger, whom I barely knew, would be driving me to the electric company in a brand-new red Ferrari to pay my bill and pay off my debt in full? God has quite a sense of humor. Who does this kind of thing? Only God does!

Chapter 3

The Earthquake and My Love for All Animals

I needed to sell the Jaguar to get a more reliable car. I was able to find a beautiful white Jeep Cherokee with palomino leather for an unbelievably low cost. This gentleman who lived in the Hollywood Hills had bought it for his daughter, and she wanted something different. So, he gave me a great deal. Only God knew that I was going to need this Jeep Cherokee for my next adventure in life.

Although I was working a full-time job, it was still not enough money to cover all the bills I had acquired and had gotten behind on. So, I sought out legal help and was advised to file bankruptcy.

I don't believe in bankruptcy, but I was advised by a pastor that, "God knows your heart and God knows that you need to start over again. He will not hold this against you." I was feeling both shame and guilt because I believed that everyone should be responsible for paying their bills. I felt filing bankruptcy would be a copout, so I originally claimed Chapter 7 bankruptcy. But then I decided to file for Chapter 11 instead, because this allows people to pay back their creditors with an affordable payment plan.

In my mind, Chapter 11 was much more acceptable for me. I'd like to say I'm not judging anyone who has had to file Chapter 7.

The trials and tribulations overwhelmed me. The "Job Journey" (named after Job in the Bible) began. Financially drained, I canceled my earthquake insurance and put my condo up for sale.

My beautiful first fur baby, Kuma

Unfortunately, two different buyers started escrow, but both had fallen through.

During these darkest, toughest years of my life, I don't know what I would have done without my beloved first dog, Kuma (the Japanese word for "Bear".) This beautiful long-haired Siberian Husky was my big, black and white, fluffy, furry angel with big blue eyes who held me when I cried and kissed my tears away. He was amazing! (Kuma was a rescue dog given to me by a director I was dating at the time.) I assumed all dogs were geniuses like Kuma. He was a gift from God. Not only did he comfort me, but he also helped save the life of my best friend, Marilyn's baby son. He got the nickname of *Park Police* because he was the advocate for all the little dogs at the dog park.

I became very passionate about dogs, and I gained a deep respect for dogs and all animals once Kuma came into my life. He actually taught me everything I needed to know about dogs and all animals. I always say that I was "doggy dumb" until Kuma came into my life.

After working long hours, little by little, I was starting to get back on my feet and able to start saving some money. I received a phone call from a friend, inviting me to attend a class with her at a local studio on "how to produce your own show." Things were starting to look up. I was even able to open an office in a Hollywood studio near Melrose for my new production company, Victory Road Productions, and started taping my TV show, *Victory Road*, featuring various celebrities. I produced eight full episodes and was presenting it to networks to buy it when suddenly, disaster struck. (More about *Victory Road* in Chapter 5.)

While going through this horrible, depressing, dark time, as if financial devastation was not enough, I found myself in the middle of the Northridge earthquake, the horrific earthquake that hit L.A. in January 1994.

As I was sleeping at 4 a.m. on January 17, 1994, I was abruptly thrown from my bed, hitting my head on a nightstand in the dark. My condo was jerking and shaking so aggressively that it sounded like a roaring lion and a train plowing through the house. Dazed and half-asleep, I quickly grabbed my dog, Kuma, and put him on a leash to prevent him from walking on the shattered glass all over the condo.

My condo had been up for sale, but it was now a complete disaster zone! Everything in it was trashed and the windows were blown out. It was as if King Kong had picked it up and shook it a few times. It looked like a bomb had exploded. I was on the first floor, and the second and third floors had crashed down on my condo.

For some strange reason, on the night before the earthquake hit, I thought it would be a cool idea to spend the night in the guest bedroom for the first time ever, just to see what it felt like to sleep in my guest bed. It was a God idea for me not to sleep in the master bedroom. Otherwise, Kuma and I both would have ended up dead. All the bedroom furniture, all the items on dressers and on the walls fell into a huge pile on top of the master bed where I normally would be sleeping. I know this was God's protection.

It is by God's grace that Kuma and I got out alive. In the midst of the shock, I scrambled around in the darkness with Kuma on his leash. To my amazement, I found a white flashlight on my kitchen counter. It was freaky. This white flashlight was not mine! I had never seen it before. It was pitch black at 4 a.m. in the morning. It had to have been placed there by the hand of God. The angels were dispatched to help bring me a light in the darkness. With that white flashlight, Kuma and I were able to help some other neighbors find their way out of the rubble.

Suddenly, I realized that Kuma and I were homeless overnight! My condo was red flagged, which means condemned and not livable. Unfortunately, I had just canceled my earthquake insurance to save money and get rid of the things I didn't think were necessary.

Once again, God made a way of escape. A friend who lived in an unaffected building down the street invited us to come and stay with her for a few days.

There were other people at her apartment who were suddenly homeless, as well. About six of us plus Kuma were sleeping on her living room floor, shaking, weary, and enduring hundreds of aftershocks. It was truly like a war zone. It was horrific. We huddled together with no running water or

With my dear friends, Matt Helreich and Sid Silver

electricity and read Psalms 91 by flashlight and candlelight. It was a time I will never forget.

A dear friend of mine who is like a brother, Sid Silver, (whom I also met through my Uncle Matt), had moved to Las Vegas, and offered for us to come stay there for a few days to decompress and breathe.

So, a few of us caravanned together to Vegas and were finally able to get some much-needed sleep and regroup.

After returning to Studio City, I had help getting my windows boarded up, and my parents flew both Kuma and me to their home in Tampa, Florida to just *breathe*. After going through that nightmare, I wasn't even sure if I was going to stay in L.A.

Kuma and I were so shell-shocked that the two of us would run to the front door at my parent's home if we heard a big truck or any booming noise. (An earthquake sounds just like a loud, roaring train.)

I had to return to L.A. and try to figure out what could be salvaged in my condo. The force of the earthquake was so strong that my jewelry was actually embedded in my white, Berber carpet. It's funny that the people who I thought would *be there* for me were absent and probably trying to recuperate themselves, and people who hardly knew me came to help.

We all had to wear leather working gloves in order to protect our hands while we sorted through all the broken glass from windows, crystal, drinking glasses, cups, plates, shattered pots, pictures, glass dining room table, etc. that were now in sharp little pieces all over the place.

God also sent my dear friend, Pastor Gregg Vernon, to help. He said he was driving by my condo building on the way to check on his parents' place, and when he saw the state that my building was in, he came up to check on me. He was shocked and actually paid some workers to help me move out a few things that could be saved such as beds, dressers, and sofa.

My friend that had offered us her place as a temporary refuge the night of the earthquake, told me that her two roommates who rented the two bedrooms upstairs, were terrified, devastated, and fled back to their hometowns.

Their understandable fear left my friend in a bind. So, she offered to rent me the huge suite upstairs that had a fireplace, outdoor deck, and a full bath. It was beautiful. I agreed to move in with my fur boy, Kuma, and start paying rent.

God was with me every step of the way and providing me with everything I needed.

When my personal manager, Brandon Kjar, found out what had happened to my place, he called and said, "Lee, I'm coming over with a big truck load of new living room furniture, curtains, paintings, decorations, dishes, and all kinds of things for your new apartment." He and his family and friends moved this huge truckload of wonderful items into my new apartment. I was in tears!

I couldn't believe my eyes! He had been to a huge estate sale and bought everything I needed. Once again, God provided all that I needed by giving me favor with various people. It was all God.

This was not a coincidence. Everything I had lost was restored with better, newer things. My new roommate loved it because her previous roommates had taken most of the furniture with them when they left. God even had her gift me with another blue-eyed, red and white, long-haired Siberian Husky named Paris. Kuma and Paris quickly became best friends and were quite the showstoppers.

Eventually, God blessed me with another roommate, who gave me her puppy Chow Chow, named Pooh Bear. She was so cute, and every little kid wanted to touch her. Kuma and Paris welcomed her as well and they quickly became fur family. I loved all my fur babies so much.

Paris

At this new apartment, I met a neighbor, Cindy Blessington (now Bauman), who lived down the hall who was also an actress. She saw my passion for animals and invited me to consider becoming her partner in the pet care business she had started.

The business was named Critter Sitters which catered to the stars and various people, and their pets.

She offered me half the business if I would help her hike, walk, and care for the dogs and cats. At first, I was not excited to walk, hike, and *scoop the poop* for other people's pets.

Pooh Bear aka Winnie the Pooh

But Cindy persuaded me to go with her one time and try it out. So, I did, and I fell in love with all the client's dogs, cats, and birds! I was so honored to be able to love and care for the pets of some of the top stars and influential people in Hollywood.

With my precious, long-haired Huskies, Kuma and Paris, they saw snow for the first time in Mt. Baldy, California

I became her partner and eventually bought her out when she was ready to retire from the pet business. I hired a staff of people, expanded to New York, and became the very first bi-coastal pet-care agency in America called L.A.– N.Y. Critter Sitters.

This business was such a blessing and grew to become highly successful. Cindy Blessington had truly *blessed me a ton* as this pet business gave me the opportunity to escape from the nightmare job at the law firm. I was still able to perform as an actress and bring in a good steady income with my passionate love for animals.

I am so amazed, as I sit here writing these life journeys, by just how much God's hand was always there, holding me and navigating me through this thing called life. Even through the sorrow and despair, HE was always there!

As I have mentioned before, God brought me this little blue-eyed, long-haired Husky and beloved angel named, Kuma, who was there in my life through the '90s, which were the darkest years of my life. Kuma eventually passed away in November 1999, at the age of twelve years old. I was devastated!

I believe that he was poisoned at the dog park by a sadistic person who left out poisoned meat to kill dogs in that park. People who lived around the park were hoping to see it close down. I believe Kuma was a statistic and a victim. I didn't know how severe it was when I took him to the vet. Then, the vet called and told me that Kuma suddenly stopped breathing and she could not revive him. He had a high level of toxicity in his liver. This was the worst news of my life at that time. He was my heart and my child, who helped me through so much sorrow. I can't wait to hold him again one day in Heaven.

Kuma was not of this world, and since he was my first dog, I didn't know that all dogs were not like him. He was truly an angel in a fur suit who comforted me every day while I went through the worst nightmare of my life.

There were times that I thought God might have forgotten me and times I felt hopeless and helpless. But He always knew the next plan He had for me, to prosper me and give me a future of hope.

Despite all the years of tears, God turned all of my scars into stars. After Kuma passed, I adopted Blue from a shelter in San Pedro in the early 2000s. Blue was a purebred, white Siberian Husky

My little boy Blue and me, after adopting him from the shelter. You can see his love and appreciation.

with blue eyes, exactly what I had been wanting in the deepest parts of my heart.

The Lord prompted a woman from a husky rescue organization to call me to tell me that there was a white Siberian Husky at the shelter who needed to be rescued that same day!

Thankfully, I was able to pick him up and take

Blue

him home that day not knowing that he was actually scheduled to be euthanized (put to death) that evening.

I recommend everyone adopt or rescue instead of buying because there are so many in need of a loving home. Thank God for animal rescues who go in and save the pets that are on death row in hopes they will be fostered and adopted.

Yes, there is a death row in every local shelter unless it is a no-kill shelter. In most states across the nation, a pet that is not rescued or adopted in seven to fourteen days is euthanized, no matter the breed.

Chapter 4

Moving to Orange County

After eight wonderful years of owning Critter Sitters, I closed it down and returned the keys to all of my clients. I had met a Christian man named David who lived in Orange County, and we started dating in 2003. We were married in 2005 and we still currently reside in O.C.

I was totally done with dating in L.A. when we met. For many years, I had dated some of the most successful men in Hollywood, including celebrities, rock stars, a real Prince, as well as a few "not so successful" men and struggling artists. For twenty years, I had chosen to remain single after an earlier divorce.

Looking back, I might have had a "bad boy syndrome." Like so many women, I may have been attracted to "bad boys," but I really wanted a man of God. As I stated earlier, I finally married a man of God.

In order to keep the L.A. Monday Night Ladies Share and Prayer Group going, I had been driving back and forth to L.A. not only for work on Films and TV, but also to continue leading and teaching the ladies group. When I moved to the O.C. (Orange County), my dear best friend, Terry Moore, generously offered to host our L.A. Share and Prayer Group meetings at her home in Santa Monica.

So, I informed the L.A. ladies that we could continue our meetings, but I would drive up monthly to lead them. Another dear, beautiful actress and model friend of mine, Terry Holbrook, also allowed us to use her gorgeous home in Malibu for a while when Terry Moore's home was unavailable.

However, things shifted in 2006 with a chain of events that were both good and not so good.

In January 2006, my Daddy, Lester Benton, passed away, just three weeks before his 86th birthday. This was so devastating and terribly sad for me. He was such a rock for our family, a strong, wise, and spiritual influence in my life. And my precious loving mommy, Earlene Benton, such a loving pillar of compassion and my best friend, was suddenly left without her beloved soul mate. They almost made it to their 60th wedding anniversary. She finally was reunited in Heaven with her Honey Bunny (a loving term of endearment she had for him), three years later.

It was another heartbreaking blow for me, but a huge blessing for her. In the midst of heartache and sorrow, God is able to pick up the shattered pieces of our hearts and put them back together again with new blessings, different blessings, in new ways.

A good thing that happened in 2006, was that my O.C. Ladies Share and Prayer Group was birthed with the same format as the L.A. Monday Night Ladies Share and Prayer Group. By this time, I had been leading, teaching, and counseling women for 16 years when God prompted me to open my home for the O.C. Ladies Share and Prayer Group. It is still going strong to this day!

In 2007, I was blessed to have my mother move to Orange County so I could help care for her while she needed full-time care at a skilled nursing facility close to my home. It was an honor to love, care, and spend quality time with my beloved mother during the last two years of her life while she rapidly declined with Alzheimer's.

By the end of 2009, my mother coherently stated that she was ready to be with Jesus and reunited with her Honey Bunny by Christmas. The Lord was kind enough to give her this Christmas wish. She was able to spend that Christmas with Jesus and her beloved husband. I was devastated and heartbroken when she passed. She was my best friend and losing both my parents within three years of each other left me feeling empty and orphaned.

Anyone who has experienced losing both parents will relate to the tremendous loss of identity and sense of feeling orphaned. You suddenly feel as if your blood lifeline, which ties you to your parenthood, is severed. It is like being held up by a parachute, and suddenly the ropes have been cut. I did not know what to do with myself, free-falling on my own without a net.

Unfortunately, I was still trying to recover from the grief of losing Paris, my sweet, long-haired red and white Husky, who passed away at the age of sixteen just two months before my mother passed. In the middle of my emptiness, despair, and grief, I adopted Starlight, a blue-eyed Husky mix who had been been rescued by the Husky Haven of L.A. Rescue, Owner Rhonda Halden, and sent to Ariel Rescue in Orange County.

She was 11 months old when I adopted her.

A couple of years later, my Chow-Chow, Pooh Bear, passed away at almost 14 years old. Blue, Starlight, and I were a team until Blue passed halfway through 2012.

I then decided to adopt another gorgeous, loving Husky named Spirit, who was also a rescue from Husky Haven of L.A. Rescue. Spirit is sable and white with golden eyes. He is so sweet and silly. He really makes me laugh.

Shortly after adopting Spirit, my dear friend, Laura DeFalco, asked us to pet sit Shadow, her little black Papillon mix while she went on a two-week vacation.

We all fell in love with this little, fun-loving, fearless fur baby and when Laura returned, she could see how happy he was here with us and the huskies. She asked if we wanted to adopt him, not knowing that I had secretly prayed while she was gone that she would allow us to keep him.

It took me two seconds to reply, "Yes"! She had six cats at home, and little Shadow was getting beaten up by one of her cats. We all agreed that this precious rescue dog would be much happier here with us.

He's the first small dog I've ever owned and a precious gift from God. He was the boss of our house, and our huskies truly loved him. We were blessed to have him in our lives. Sadly, he passed away from kidney disease in May 2022, a week after his 14th birthday. I really miss that little angel.

Our fur crew today consists of our precious huskies, Starlight and Spirit. They are both seniors now and I have decided to give them my undivided attention before adopting anymore.

64

RSVP to Heaven by Lee Benton

A Time of Reflection

I look back and think about how the O.C. Ladies Share and Prayer Group would always thank me for opening my home to them. However, I needed them more than they needed me. Hard times are hard times, but you can survive if you don't give up. The devil wanted me to quit, because he knew my real purpose was right around the corner. He knew this original L.A. Monday Night Share and Prayer Group was going to flourish and turn into a worldwide ministry.

In 2012, the Lord broadened my ministry to teach both men and women at CBS Studios. I was having a moment with God about opening the group to men as we started to grow, because I was used to counseling only women and felt inadequate and unequipped to include men. Then I asked God, "Why me, God? Who is going to listen to me? I feel I am so imperfect." Then God told me, "I need an imperfect person to teach an imperfect world." Every time I feel like I am ill-equipped or feel like hiding, He keeps reminding me of this truth.

The group grew from the L.A. Monday Night Ladies Share and Prayer Group and had blossomed into my O.C. Ladies Share and Prayer Group, then expanded into my worldwide ministry, Lee Benton Ministries International.

We had producers, directors, actors, singers, recording artists, writers, musicians, agents, doctors, lawyers, and many other diverse professionals.

We were blessed to have CBS Studios allow us to use a building on their lot to hold our non-denominational monthly service for six years until they eventually needed our building, after which we moved to a large theater in Hollywood.

We are currently meeting in another location. If you're ever in L.A., I welcome you to visit us. You can find out where our monthly meetings are being held on my website at: LeeBenton.org

I had never put much value on titles until I was asked in 2014 to officiate a private celebrity's wedding that was so exclusive, the world could not know about it.

To officiate this wedding, I had to become an officially ordained pastor. Since then, I've had the honor of officiating weddings, baptisms, and baby dedications as well as funerals (which is always hard for me).

Throughout the years, I have maintained my acting career. I've continually starred in and played supporting roles in various films and TV shows. I found out that I can keep my passion for acting while doing God's work.

Chapter 5

VICTORY ROAD TV Show
Resurrected and Transformed

In 2014, I was asked to be a guest on a TV show and be interviewed on a network outside of L.A. I was introduced to the founder of the network.

Afterward, I prayed with him and shared with him that I had produced a show but had put it aside after the 1994 earthquake.

I thought my dream of *VICTORY ROAD* had passed me by and gave up on it after 20 years. At that point, God said to resurrect the dream. The network founder invited me to join his network with a discounted fee. It was time to bring *VICTORY ROAD* back to life, but with a new title, *VICTORY ROAD with Lee Benton*!

Again, this is just God at work. He wants to give us the desires of our heart, but He requires something from us first. He asks that we put Him first, then He will give us the desires of our heart.

When I first produced my TV show in 1994, I did not have the access to the whole world that I did in 2014. This meant that God did not take away my dream. He only paused it for a while to promote it on a much larger scale to the entire world through satellite, live streaming, and many other incredible platforms.

When God rebirthed it He gave my dream back to me and on a much larger scale. Sometimes God's "no" either protects us or pauses us for a much bigger vision, a much bigger dream than we could ever imagine. His delay was for my good and for His greater glory to the masses. He has a vast domain with storehouses full of blessings stored in heaven for each of us individually. He is ready to pour them out on us in His perfect timing.

I answered the call to resurrect my show, His show, and I started doing tapings. I did live tapings there for a year and a half. After that, the Lord opened larger doors at other networks. I welcome everyone to go to LeeBenton.org and view all the previously aired programs.

In the same year, I was awarded a "Merit of Honor" from the president of the United States for all the volunteer work I had done to help others. I was also given a "Merit of Honor" from the Order of St. Lazarus of Jerusalem for my ministry work in God's Kingdom.

In 2015, the United Nations awarded me the "Goodwill Ambassador" award by the Golden Rule Organization.

After that, I was blessed to receive a Doctorate of Theology in 2017 from Next Dimension University, which also honored me in 2019 with the Lifetime Achievement Award. The recognition and awards are nice, but to God be all the glory!

Actress Terry Moore and me each accepting our
Lifetime Achievement Awards in August 2019

In 2019, VICTORY ROAD with Lee Benton was
nominated for Best TV Show, and God blessed me
with the Best TV Show Host Award from ICFF—
International Christian Film Festival. This truly was a
Cinderella moment, because I was up against some of
the strongest and most incredible TV shows across the
world. It was the global Oscars for faith-based TV
shows, films, and music. People attended from all
over the world.

Once I realized how many TV shows I was up against, it was very nerve-racking. Before they called my name, my husband, David, leaned over and said, "Do you have an acceptance speech prepared?" I looked at him startled and dazed, saying "No." He asked, "Why not?" I responded, "Because I work day and night and didn't have time to write a speech." Then suddenly the master of ceremonies on stage said, "And, the winner is . . . Lee Benton from VICTORY ROAD with Lee Benton TV Show." It felt like a dream! I was not expecting it at all. I was hoping my entire team would win with me for Best TV Show.

So, I was sitting there in shock when they called my name for Best TV Host. I finally stood up and felt like I was floating. I couldn't even find the stage. I needed to be directed to the stage. I was taking so long to find the steps to the stage that the announcer was about to accept the award on my behalf. It was all a blur. I had a Lucille Ball moment until I was finally on the stage. Then, I realized I still had no speech prepared and thought, "What am I going to say?" I was not expecting to win this award at all. I looked out into the audience wondering, "What am I doing here? What just happened?

After receiving the award for Best TV Host at ICFF –
International Christian Film Festival

Anything that came out of my mouth must have come straight from the Holy Spirit, because I had no idea what I was saying. You can check out the magical moment on my website.

I was then quickly escorted to the back of the stage and rushed over to another room on the red carpet to talk to paparazzi, take pictures, and be interviewed. I eventually found my way back to the audience while other awards were being given.

I sat there stunned with the award in my hand. I looked down and silently prayed, "Father God, thank you for this award and I'm so grateful for this and I really appreciate it, but why didn't I win the award for Best TV Show?" The Holy Spirit then whispered to me, 'If you had won for Best TV Show, it would have been for everyone. I wanted you to have Best TV Host because this was for YOU personally, for all of your years of hard work and faithfulness.'

At that moment, I realized that He wanted to give me a personal hug. I wanted kudos for my team, but He wanted to acknowledge all my years of labor and sacrifice for Him. I share all these mentionable honors with you not to be braggadocious but to encourage you. While you might be going through certain storms like the ones I experienced during my decade of sorrows, I want you to know God can turn it all around and give you a brand-new tomorrow.

If you check out my show, you will see at the end of each episode that I share a special prayer that the Lord gave me to share with the whole world. I use every opportunity with every guest appearance I make, and on every interview I do, to share this prayer. I call it the "RSVP Prayer to Heaven."

Chapter 6

The RSVP Prayer

Now that you have had a little peek into my life, I would like to share that after having said all of this, I have learned to fully put my trust and faith in God alone. I realize that my journey of trials and tribulations, heartache, and sorrow, was to groom me because He had much more work for me to do in the future. He had a bigger purpose, a bigger plan, for my life.

Just like a palm tree that blows in the wind, each storm and each blow make the roots grow deeper and stronger, enabling us to withstand the greater storms that life may present. Not all of us are called to be generals in God's army, so not everyone goes through the same depth of sorrows and trials. It depends on their calling in life. There are different levels in God's army, but God knew that with His help, I would become the warrior that he needed and the mouthpiece for Him to speak to the world.

The Lord told me that heaven is like any nice event here on earth. Anytime you get invited to any nice event, such as a banquet, a wedding, or even a nice restaurant, you have to RSVP to get your name on the guest list and to have a reserved seat. If you don't, you just don't get in. He also asked me to tell you that no matter what race or what religion, He wants everyone to RSVP out of your own mouth, so He can save you a seat and put your name in His big reservation book! It is called the Lamb's Book of Life.

So, I sit here writing this book and revisiting my life thus far, not for me, but for you.

I would like to invite you to pray this simple "RSVP Prayer to Heaven," so that in the end of days, your name will be in God's big reservation book. And, you will have a reserved seat in heaven with your name on it.

So, this is my question for you . . . are you ready to reserve your seat? Do you really know if your name is on God's guest list? Please pray this prayer with me and know that this is the most important prayer that you will ever pray in your entire life. God saved my life to share this prayer with you and to help save your life, too.

Please pray this RSVP prayer, which has been composed in English. We also have it in many other translations which can be accessed by going to my website at: www.leebenton.org and click on RSVP Prayer. You can download it and share it directly with your family and friends.

RSVP to God's Invitation to Heaven

When you are invited to a special event or party, you need to RSVP, or your name will not be on the guest list, and you will not be able to get in. (Reservations need to be made ahead of time to reserve yourself a seat). God's Kingdom is the same. Unless you RSVP to Him (responding to His invitation in the Bible)— you will not have a reserved seat in Heaven. It is just that simple.

No matter what race or religion, we must individually reply to God's invite.

The 3 A's to Accepting Jesus Christ:
- Admit you are a sinner (we all have sinned).
- Accept Jesus died on the Cross for your sins.
- Ask Him to come into your Heart and be your Lord and Savior.

The RSVP Prayer

Father God, I come to you a sinner . . . please forgive me of my sins as I forgive all those who have sinned against me.

I believe that Jesus is the Christ, the Son of the Living God who died for me and arose for me so that I could spend eternity with you.

Please put my name in your book and reserve me a seat, as I follow you all the days of my life.

Thank you for my salvation, in Jesus' name, Amen.

"If you confess with your mouth and believe in your heart that God has raised Him [Jesus] from the dead, you shall be saved."
(Romans 10:9)

Copyright 2014

You can use the QR Code provided below to access all the various translations. If you do not see the language that you need, please let us know by sending us a translation request to: Lee@LeeBenton.org and we will gladly add it!

To scan this RSVP Prayer QR Code:

1. Open the Camera app on your phone.
2. Hold your phone over the QR Code, so that it's clearly visible within your phone's screen.
3. When you correctly hold your phone over a QR Code, your phone automatically scans the code, or it will ask you to press a button to snap a picture.

Acknowledgments

First, I want to thank God my Heavenly Father, Jesus Christ my Savior, King, and my precious Holy Spirit.

My husband David — Thank you for all the years of love and faithful support you have given me, both personally and financially in my ministry. I am so grateful and thankful that you have consistently helped me through the years with my ministry in L.A., and continually bless me with your prayers, tithes, and generous offerings to help spread the Gospel across the world.

I'm so grateful and thankful for my sister Carolyn Chandler and for every one of my beloved family members.

My little Granny Vetzel, who loved the Lord and gave her all for the family with a bigger than life personality. (She could have been an actress). We had so much fun traveling together. She would make me laugh so hard, always baked my favorite bread pudding and, while blind in one eye, managed to write me the most amazing, loving letters when I first moved away to California. I still have every letter. I miss her so much.

My other grandparents, Grandma and Grandpa Benton, were also godly and loving. Grandma Benton always cooked a feast for all of our huge family reunions. I loved her special dumplings and blackberry cobbler. She always made a birthday cake for Jesus at Christmas, and we all sang Happy Birthday to Him. I remember

Grandma holding me on her lap and singing songs. She had a huge toy box filled with toys for all the grandkids to enjoy. Grandpa Benton was a real jokester, making us laugh while passing out his favorite Juicy Fruit Gum. Such great memories!

I'd also like to give a special thanks to my cousin, Wanda McDonell, and Aunt Elouise Allen for their love, prayers, and endless trips to the cemetery to take flowers and groom my precious parents' graves in my absence. God bless you!

To my Aunt Annie Lee Vetzel, who always sent me cards and words of encouragement for many years just when I needed it most. So timely, so precious!

I'm also very thankful to every one of you who has constantly lifted me up in prayers, donated your time, talents, generous donations, love, and support for my ministry through the years. I couldn't have done this journey without you. You truly have made a huge difference in my personal life, career, and ministry. I love you all from the depths of my heart, and I'm so blessed to have you in my life!

Millie Gates — My O.C. bestie, loving prayer partner, and huge financial supporter in my ministry. I'm forever grateful!

Emma Rose Roldan Klinger — My former Executive Assistant who is studying to be a doctor, and encouraged me and worked tirelessly to help me "get the book done."

My original team from Lee Benton Ministries International at CBS Studios and *VICTORY ROAD with Lee Benton TV Show*, *Mr. Jones and The LBM Band*, *Victory Road Band*, and dear friends:

Philip R. Jones — Worship Director, Singer, Songwriter, and Recording Artist.

Sheryl Helene Wilson — Worship Leader, Singer, Songwriter and Recording Artist. Sheryl tours with the fabulous band, Machaira, and with Gospel Recording Artist, Leon Patillo, formerly of Santana.

Anthony Salerno — Musician, Singer, Songwriter, Producer, Director, and Director of Photography

I'm blessed to have my current Worship Director, Lyn LiVigni. And thanks also to Marcos Lopez-Iglesias, and the talented *LBM Band.*

Marianne Ricci — Faithful, dedicated marathon warrior, friend, and supporter of my ministry.

Beka Ricci — Faithful friend, beloved survivor, Actress, and supporter of my ministry.

Cathy Newton — Dear friend, Speaker, Interpretive Dancer, and owner of *Role Models* and founder of *The Voice of Fire Ministry*, who prays, cares, and helped me through my darkest years.

Trish Steele — Founder, *"Safe Passage Heals"*, *Women Crowned in Glory*, and *"Women of Steele,"* Speaker,

Author of *Discover the Mind of Steele*, and dear friend who made it possible to hold my church services at CBS Studios and supporter of my ministry.

Pastor/Evangelist Betty Green Suddreth -- *Betty Green Ministries*, mentor, Author of many books, and beloved friend who ordained me.

Mel Novak — Actor, Evangelist, Prison Minister, Skid Row Minister, and dear friend who has always been there for me through the years.

Dr. Joel McLeod — Founder and Chancellor of *Next Dimension University*, Evangelist, Pastor, Author of many books, and dear friend.

Bill Cline — Faithful, dedicated friend and Cameraman for many years at my L.A. ministry.

Catherine Dyment — Assistant for my TV show and L.A. Ministry for over ten years, dear friend, and supporter.

Sara (Zari) Daraie, Author of *Lost Refugees Found In Christ,* and her daughter Roya Daraie (Ortega) – dear friends who support both me and my ministry.

Dr. Catherine Maloof, Rosie Maloof, and Maureen Maloof, Founder of *Uniforms for Hope* – dear friends who always have my back and support my ministry.

Susie Palmer and Cindy Morales – Thank you my dear friends, for all of your love and support to my ministry.

Kelly Gallaher, daughter Chloe, and Kelly's mom, Judy Todd Yandura, thank you for your love and financial support to my ministry.

Sheryl Helene Wilson and Jan Wilson – my dear friends, thank you for your love and financial support to my ministry.

Debra Newell — Designer, Speaker, Author of *Surviving Dirty John*, domestic violence advocate, my dear friend and financial supporter of my ministry.

To all of my O.C. Ladies Share and Prayer Group and monthly prayer warriors since 2006 . . . I love you all!

Joanna (Angel) Hairabedian and husband David — Authors, Evangelists, Producers, Hosts of *Virtual Church Media,* and *Prison Bible Ministry.* Joanna is a Musical Worshiper and former Ms. America, (my besties and prayer partners). David's Bestseller, *Jet Ride to Hell.* Joanna's book is *The 7 Mistakes That Women Make That Repel Good Men and How to Reverse Them.* Her Podcast is *Reveal the Diamond Within.*

Kimberly Bradford and family — My dear friend and family of pastors in Ohio who pray for me daily.

Shelley Abblett and husband Don — Faithful supporters of my ministry. She's been my best friend since I was 18 years old, former model and agent who knows all my secrets!

Kimberly Feazell — My niece in Florida, who has always shown me love and supported me while going through her own pain and trials.

Jan Morris — Former Writer/PR for Sony Pictures and dear friend who always has my back.

Mickey Sinardi — Writer, Journalist, Performer, and dear friend who I call *"my brother from another mother"* who I've known since elementary school.

Gary Kirkland — My loving, lifetime friend and big brother from school and church.

Tony Zappone — Journalist, photographer, dear friend who helped catapult my 10-year modeling career with his amazing photography & first modeling composite.

Leah Latini — Owner, *Marketing to Scale, who is my* marketing expert and website designer for both my TV Show and worldwide ministry. She has been a generous supporter of my ministry and friend. Thank you to Sara (Zari) Daraie for the introduction. I'm so grateful.

Hope Kelley — Publisher, *Hope Kelley Book Publishing,* owner of *ECBYBooks Bookstore*, Actress, Artist/Illustrator, Producer, and Author of many books who has been my dear friend for forty years. Not only did she publish this book, but she encouraged me to do so.

Lara Magallon — Founder, *Dogaholics* and Author of many books (her latest is *The Heavenly Dog Father Prayer Book I* and *II*), loving friend, and advocate for dogs.

Bob Goodman — Book Editor and friend who has patiently taught me a lot about writing.

Dr. Bita Badakshan — Integrative Medicine and Family Practitioner and personal friend who helped save my life and truly cares about my well-being.

René Alt — Hair Stylist and Makeup Artist, and dear friend who volunteered her time and talent to work on my TV show.

Nina Saylor Lowe — My best friend since 5th grade. I miss you terribly. (Deceased, 2023)

Mazie Aubrey Young — My high school teacher and friend who taught business administration and typing and made such an impact on my life. I miss you! (Deceased, 2017)

Myra Cain Groover — My high school teacher who taught me shorthand and bookkeeping. I still use these skills every day.

Mari Nihei — Actress, spokesperson, business owner, and dear friend who made my ministry conference in Japan possible.

AUTHOR, MODEL, ACTRESS, PRODUCER, EVANGELIST
AND ADVOCATE FOR ANIMALS

"Life"
by Lee Benton

Life…it is here for but a moment with those we love so dear,
the ones with whom we share our thoughts,
who comfort every tear.
It may leave as the breath of the mighty winds,
gone forever from our reach,
just as a pebble is cast into the endless sea,
leaving the shore of a troubled beach.

"For I am not ashamed of the Gospel of Christ,
for it is the power of God unto salvation for everyone who believes…"
Romans 1:16